A White Heron

and Other American Short Stories

Level 2

Retold by Mary Gladwin
Series Editors: Andy Hopkins and Jocelyn Potter

D1563077

Pearson Education Limited
Edinburgh Gate, Harlow,
Essex CM20 2JE, England
and Associated Companies throughout the world.

ISBN 0 582 43049 6

This selection of stories first published 2000

Text copyright © Penguin Books 2000
Illustrations copyright © Luigi Galante (Virgil Pomfret) 2000

Typeset by Digital Type, London
Set in 11/14pt Bembo
Printed in Spain by Mateu Cromo, S. A. Pinto (Madrid)

Published by Pearson Education Limited in association with
Penguin Books Ltd, both companies being subsidiaries of Pearson Plc

For a complete list of the titles available in the Penguin Readers series please write to your local
Pearson Education office or to: Marketing Department, Penguin Longman Publishing,
5 Bentinck Street, London W1M 5RN.

Contents

Introduction

He waits for her story. She can't tell him! But why can't she speak? She is nine years old, and he is her first friend. Is the bird more important than him?

A White Heron, the first story in this book, is about a little girl. Sylvia's only friends are birds and animals. But then one day a stranger comes. He is a new friend, but he likes to kill birds. Will Sylvia tell him about the white heron?

In *The Story of an Hour,* a young woman lives through an hour of her life. Is there something more important than love? *The Complete Life of John Hopkins* is about people in the Big City. What really makes their life complete? *Luck* is the story of a famous Englishman. Is he a great man? His teacher tells a different story. In *The Tell-Tale Heart,* a man is very afraid. What is he planning? And will it really help him?

These stories are by five great American writers.

Sarah Orne Jewett (1849–1909) wrote about country life in New England. She wrote *A White Heron* in 1886. Her most famous book is *The Country of the Pointed Firs* (1896).

Kate O'Flaherty Chopin (1850-1904) wrote *The Story of an Hour* in 1899. In *Bayou Folk* (1894) and *A Night In Acadie* (1897), she wrote about the people of Louisiana.

O. Henry (William Sydney Porter, 1862–1919) lived in New York when he wrote *The Complete Life of John Hopkins* in 1908. He wrote around 300 stories.

Mark Twain (Samuel Langhorne Clemens, 1835–1910) wrote *Luck* after he visited Europe in 1867. He also wrote *The Adventures of Tom Sawyer* (1876) and *The Adventures of Huckleberry Finn* (1884); these are Penguin Readers.

Edgar Allan Poe (1809–49) wrote *The Tell-Tale Heart* in 1843. There is a Penguin Readers book of his stories too: *The Fall of the House of Usher and Other Stories.*

A White Heron

Sarah Orne Jewett

It was about eight o'clock on a June evening. The sun shone between the trees, but it was almost dark in the woods. A little girl walked home slowly with her cow. They walked away from the light into the woods. They couldn't see the way, but their feet knew it.

Every evening in summer, Sylvia had to look for the old cow. The cow didn't want to go back to the farm. Sylvia called her, but the cow didn't come. She stood very quietly, and she didn't make a sound. Sometimes Sylvia got tired of the game.

The cow was a difficult animal, but she was a good friend. She gave a lot of good milk. When the weather was warm, Sylvia liked the game. Also, she had a lot of time. "She wants to play with me," the little girl thought. She didn't have other friends, so she happily played with the cow.

But the game was very long that night. This time, the cow got tired first. She called to Sylvia. The little girl laughed when she found her near the river.

It was late, and the old cow wanted to go home. She turned onto the farm road and walked quickly in front of Sylvia.

Sylvia thought about her grandmother. "What will she say?" she thought. "I left home at half past five."

But Mrs. Tilley knew the old cow. Before Sylvia came to the farm, Mrs. Tilley had to look for the cow every evening. Now she waited at home and thought about Sylvia. "She's a good girl," she thought. "Sometimes she comes back late, but that's all right. I know that she likes walking in the woods. She couldn't do that when she lived in the town."

1

Mrs. Tilley remembered Sylvia's first day at the farm. The child was eight years old, one of her daughter's many children. "She's afraid of people," they said.

"That won't be a problem," Mrs. Tilley thought. "There aren't many people around the farm."

When she and Sylvia arrived at the house, only the cat met them. It was happy because its stomach was full of young birds. "This is a beautiful place!" thought Sylvia. "I'll never want to go home."

The young girl and the cow walked through the woods. The cow stopped and drank from a small river. Sylvia stood in the water and listened happily to the birds. She heard noises in the branches above her head. The trees were full of little birds and animals. Some animals moved around at night, but other animals slept.

Sylvia wanted to sleep too, but she was almost home. She wasn't usually in the woods as late as this, but she felt happy.

She thought about the town. "I left there last year," she thought. "Is everything the same now?" She thought about a big boy with a red face. When she lived in the town, he often ran after her. She was afraid of him. When she thought about him, she walked quickly through the dark woods.

Suddenly, the little girl heard a whistle. It wasn't a bird's whistle—it was a boy's whistle. It was very loud and very near. Sylvia left the cow and ran behind a big tree.

Somebody spoke to her in a friendly way. "Hello, little girl," he said. "Is the road near here?"

A young man with a gun stood in front of Sylvia. She didn't look at him, but she answered, "No, it isn't." She was afraid, but she came out from behind the tree. She followed the cow, and he walked with her.

"I'm looking for birds," said the young man kindly, "and I can't find the road. Don't be afraid. What's your name? Can I stay at

"I'm looking for birds," said the young man kindly, "and I can't find the road."

your house tonight? Then I'll go shooting tomorrow morning."

Sylvia was more afraid then. She thought about her grandmother. "What will she say? Will she be angry? Did I do something wrong?" she thought.

He asked her name again. She looked at the ground, but she answered the young man. "Sylvy," she said very quietly.

Mrs. Tilley came outside when they arrived. The cow called loudly to her.

"Where did she go this time, Sylvy?" she asked. Sylvia didn't answer. She was afraid. Her grandmother didn't understand.

"Does she think he's a neighbor?" she thought. "We don't know him."

The young man put down his gun and his bag next to the door. "Good evening," he said to Mrs. Tilley. He told his story again. He wanted to stay there that night.

"I have to leave early tomorrow morning," he said. "I'll sleep anywhere, but I'm very hungry. I know that you can give me some milk."

"Yes, of course," answered Mrs. Tilley kindly. "There are better places on the big road, but you can stay here. Come in and sit down. I'll get the milk. Sylvy! Go and get a plate for the young man!"

The young man was surprised. The little house in the New England woods was clean and nice. "It's better than a lot of other houses," he thought.

He listened happily to the old woman and he watched Sylvia's little face and her gray eyes. "That was a very good dinner," he told them. "I don't often eat as well as that." After dinner, the new friends sat down outside and looked at the night sky.

Mrs. Tilley talked, and he listened. "The wild fruit will be ready in few weeks. Sylvy will help me bring it back from the woods. The cow gives us a lot of milk, but she's difficult. She always runs away."

She told him about her family. "Four of my children died," she said. "Now I only have Sylvia's mother and a son. My son, Dan, lives in California, or he's dead. I don't know. Dan loved shooting. When he was home, he always brought me birds and little animals. He likes to move around, but he doesn't like to write letters."

The old woman was quiet for a minute. "Sylvy's the same as him," she said with a smile. "She knows every tree in the woods. The birds and animals know her well. They come and eat from her hand. She gave them too much of her food, so I stopped her. And Dan had a bird too. It stayed here after he left. He and his father had angry words, and Dan left. His father was sad about that."

The young man stopped listening. He wanted to ask a question. "Does Sylvy know much about birds?" he asked. He looked at the quiet little girl. "I like catching birds," he said. "I started when I was a boy. I'm looking for two or three different birds now, but it isn't easy."

"What do you do with them?" asked Sylvia's grandmother. "Do you have a farm?"

"Oh, no," he answered. "My birds are all dead. I put them on shelves in my house. I have a lot of them. I catch them or I shoot them."

He looked at Sylvia. "I saw a white heron near here on Saturday," he said. "It came this way and I followed it. They don't usually live around here. It's a little white heron." Sylvia didn't look at him, and she didn't say anything. She watched the cat.

"Do you know this bird?" the young man asked excitedly. "It's a strange, tall white bird with long, thin legs. It makes a nest high up in a tree."

Sylvia's heart jumped. She remembered that strange bird. It stood in an open place between the river and the woods. The sunlight was yellow and warm, and the ground was green and wet.

The young man spoke again. "I want to find that white

heron," he said. "I'll look for it all summer, and somebody will have to help me. I'll pay that person ten dollars."

Mrs. Tilley was surprised when she heard this. Sylvia didn't say anything. She looked at the cat again. It wanted to go into the house. It was usually quiet at this time of night, but now there were too many people. Sylvia thought about the ten dollars. She wanted a lot of things. "How many things can ten dollars buy?" she thought.

The next day, the young man walked in the woods with Sylvia. She wasn't afraid of him now, because he was kind and friendly. He told her interesting things about birds, and he gave her a wonderful knife.

She was only afraid when he shot a bird. "Why does he do that?" she thought. "He says that he likes birds." But she liked him very much. She watched him with a heart full of love.

They walked quietly through the woods. They stopped and listened to a bird's song. They looked through the branches excitedly. They didn't speak often, and they spoke quietly.

Sylvia was sad because they didn't find the white heron. She didn't show the young man the way, because she only followed him. She never spoke first. She only answered "yes" or "no."

When evening came, they walked home with the cow. Sylvia smiled happily when she saw a big tree. "He whistled here last night and I was afraid," she thought.

In an open place near the woods, there was a very big tree. It was bigger than the other trees. Sylvia knew it well. She often put her hand on it, and looked up. The wind always moved those branches when it was hot on the ground.

"One morning, I'll climb up to the top of this tree," she thought excitedly. "I'll see the ocean and the world! I'll see the white heron's nest! And then I'll tell him!" She was very happy when she thought about that wonderful day.

The door of the little house was open all night. Birds came to it and sang. The young man and the old woman were asleep. Sylvia watched and waited. She forgot about sleep. She thought only about her plan. For her, the short summer night was as long as a dark winter night. Then the songs of the birds stopped. "Is it morning?" she thought.

She quietly left the house and walked quickly through the woods. She woke up some birds and they made little noises. They were friendly sounds, and she felt happy. But she had a new friend in her life now. Was he more important than her friends in the woods?

She arrived at the open place. The big tree was asleep in the dark. It was almost as high as the sky.

Little Sylvia began to climb a smaller tree next to it, because the big tree didn't have any branches near the ground. She was very excited. She used her fingers and her feet and she climbed up through the wet, dark branches. A bird flew up out of its nest. She felt her way easily because she knew this tree well. Its high branches were next to the big tree.

She climbed onto a long branch, and then jumped across to the big tree. It was very hard, and the branches hurt her thin little fingers. She climbed around and up the big tree. The birds in the woods below began to sing. It was lighter near the top of the tree. She climbed quickly because it was almost morning.

The little girl climbed higher and higher. The big tree was surprised when it felt the little girl in its branches. It carefully moved its smallest branches and put them under her feet. It wanted to help this light little person. It stopped the wind for her. The old tree loved its new friend. It loved her more than the birds and animals in the woods. She was small and weak, but she wasn't afraid.

When the sun came up early in the east on that June morning, Sylvia stood at the top of the tree. She was tired but excited. She could see the blue ocean and the morning sun.

Two big birds flew in the east, in front of the sun. They looked dark in the blue sky. They flew high above the ground, but below the top of the tree. Sylvia wanted to fly away with them. To the west, she could see woods, farms, and towns. It was a big, exciting world!

The birds sang loudly, and the sunlight was now very strong. Sylvia could see ships on the ocean. The world looked wonderful from the top of the tree, but she couldn't see the heron's nest. "Where is it?" she thought. "The ocean is beautiful, but I have to find that nest!"

She looked down at the branches and then at a green open place between the trees. Suddenly, she saw something small and white near an old dead tree. It moved and got bigger. It was the heron!

It flew up near the big old tree. The little girl didn't move a foot or a finger. "Can it see me?" she thought. "Can it feel my eyes on it? Does it know that I'm thinking about it?"

The heron flew into a smaller tree and sat there. It called back to its nest in the old dead tree. A second heron answered.

A minute later, a large number of other birds flew into the tree. They called loudly and flew from branch to branch. The heron flew away, back to its nest. Sylvia felt sad, but also happy. "Now I know!" she thought excitedly.

She followed the same dangerous way down again. She put her feet carefully on one branch after the other. She couldn't look down. Sometimes she wanted to cry, because her hands and her feet hurt. One time, she almost fell.

She thought about the young man many times. "What will he think when I tell him about the heron's nest? What will he say?"

"Sylvy, Sylvy!" called her busy old grandmother again and again. Nobody answered, and Sylvia wasn't in her little bed.

It was the heron!

The young man woke up and quickly put on his clothes. He thought about this new day and about the quiet little girl. "I watched her yesterday when I talked about the heron's nest," he thought. "She knows about it, and she'll tell me today. She has to tell me!"

◆

Then Sylvia arrives home. Her old dress and her hands and feet are dirty.

Her grandmother and the young man wait at the door. They ask her the question. The little girl thinks about the dead tree and the open green place, but she doesn't answer.

Her grandmother looks angry, and the young man looks sad. He asks her the question kindly and looks into her eyes. He talks about money. Sylvia knows that her grandmother doesn't have much money. She wants the young man to be happy. But she doesn't answer. He waits for her story.

She can't tell him! But why can't she speak? She is nine years old, and he is her first friend. Is the bird more important than him?

She hears the sound of the wind in the green branches, and she remembers the white heron. She watched the ocean and the morning with the heron. She cannot tell its story and give its life away.

◆

The young man wasn't happy when he went away later that day. Sylvia felt very sad too. She wanted to be his friend and to love him.

At night, she often heard his whistle in the woods when she came home with the old cow. She heard his gun. Then she saw the little dead birds fall to the ground. She felt sad because he wasn't her friend.

She can't tell him!

So I ask you, the woods and the summer time, "Did she do the right thing? Who was a better friend, the heron or the man? Remember this little child of the woods. She lost a friend for you, so please be kind to her!"

The Story of an Hour

Kate Chopin

Mrs. Mallard had a weak heart, so her sister Josephine was very careful. She spoke slowly and quietly. She didn't tell her everything, but she had to tell her. Her husband was dead.

Her husband's friend Richards was there too. He knew about the train accident, because he was in the newspaper office at the time. He saw the names of the dead, with Brently Mallard's name at the top. He went quickly to her sister's house and told her.

When Mrs. Mallard understood, she cried suddenly and wildly in her sister's arms. Then she stopped. She left them and went to her room. She didn't want them to follow her.

There was a big armchair in her room, next to an open window. She was very tired, and she sat down heavily.

She could see an open square outside her window. It was spring, and the trees were green. There was a light wind. "It's going to rain," she thought. Birds sang in the trees. The sky was dark over the square, but it was blue in the west.

She sat in the chair and she didn't move. She began to cry again, and then she sat quietly.

She was young, and her face was pretty and quiet. It was a strong face, but now there was no light in her eyes. She looked out at the blue sky, but her eyes saw nothing. She didn't want to think.

She waited for something, and she felt afraid. What was it? She didn't know its name, but she could feel it. It came in through the open window with the sounds and colors.

It came nearer, and then she knew its name. She tried to stop it, but it was too strong. The idea came and stayed.

"Free, free, free!"

Her mouth opened, and one quiet word came out. She repeated it again and again: "Free, free, free!" She wasn't afraid now. The light came back into her eyes. Her heart felt strong and her body felt warm. She was happy now. Was that bad? She didn't think about it. It wasn't important.

She thought about her husband, and remembered his face. "I know that I'll cry again," she thought. "I'll be sad when I see him. He always looked at me with love, and now he's cold and gray and dead."

But then she thought about the future. "It's mine!" she thought. "Those days and years are all mine." She opened her arms to those days. "I'll be free," she thought. "Nobody will tell me, 'Do this! Don't do that!' Why do people say that? Sometimes they're kind, but it isn't right."

Her husband was a good man, but she wasn't free. She sometimes loved him, but often she didn't. Love wasn't important now. She felt something stronger. She felt free! She said the same words again and again: "Free! Free!"

Her sister Josephine came to her room and spoke to her. "Louise! Open the door! Please! Louise, are you sick?"

"Go away! I'm fine!" said Louise. She was very well. Her new life came in through the open window, and it brought her hope. She thought about the future again. She saw spring days and summer days. "Those days will be mine!" she thought. "Only yesterday, I wanted a short life, but now I want it to be very long!"

She stood up and opened the door for her sister. Her eyes shone. Her head was high when she walked. She took her sister's arm and they went down the stairs. Richards waited for them at the bottom.

Then somebody opened the door. It was Brently Mallard, home from the train station. He didn't know about the accident. He wasn't there when it happened.

Josephine screamed. Richards moved quickly in front of Brently Mallard's wife, but he was too late.

"It was her heart," said the doctors, later. "She was too happy, and it killed her."

The Complete Life of John Hopkins

O. Henry

What are the most important things in life? You have to fall in love. You have to go to war. You have to be poor. Nobody's life is complete without these three things.

But do you also have to be rich? Is that as important as the other things? No, it isn't. A poor man is very happy when he finds a dollar. A rich man can't understand this.

Everybody in the world has to have these three things. In the country, they aren't very important. You don't have to have a lot of money. Love is not as strong as it is in the city. Wars are smaller. People only fight about little things. But in the city, they are more important. John Hopkins learned this in a very short time.

The Hopkins apartment was the same as a thousand other apartments. There were some flowers in one window. An old dog sat in the other window and waited.

John Hopkins was the same as a thousand other men. He went to work every day, and every week he brought home twenty dollars. He worked in an office on the ninth floor. What did he do? We don't know.

Mrs. Hopkins was the same as a thousand other women. She liked to stay at home, but she also liked to go out on Sunday afternoons. She always bought food at the same store, and she paid for it later. She liked to go shopping when things were cheap. She didn't like her neighbor on the third floor. She looked out the window for hours, and she listened to the sounds in the street. She was the same as every woman in an apartment in the Big City.

In the Big City, important things happen, and they happen

quickly. You meet an old friend from school in the street. You go for a walk in the park with your friend. Somebody hits you on the head and takes your money. You go to the hospital. You meet a girl and you marry her. Then she leaves you. You lose your job. You meet a rich girl. Everything happens very fast.

You walk through the streets, and somebody calls your name. You find something on the ground, or something falls on your head. You have an accident or you lose your money. You fight with a waiter, or you fight with your wife.

John Hopkins sat in his apartment after a small dinner. He sat in an armchair and looked at an ugly picture on the wall. Mrs. Hopkins told a boring story about the neighbors, but he didn't listen. The old dog looked at him in a very unfriendly way and showed its yellow teeth.

There was no love or war in this apartment, and they weren't poor. Life wasn't complete, but there was hope.

John Hopkins wanted to say something interesting. "There's a new man at work," he said.

"Oh, really?" said Mrs. Hopkins. She wasn't very interested.

"Mr. Whipple wore his new coat today," he said. "I liked it. It's gray and . . ."

An idea came to him and he stopped suddenly. "I'm going to the store. I want a cigar," he said. He put on his hat and coat, and he walked out the door and down the stairs.

It was a warm evening, and the streets were full of small children. The older boys and girls talked on the stairs. Their parents stood in the doorways and looked out at the street.

John Hopkins walked into Mr. Freshmayer's cigar store for the first time. Mr. Freshmayer didn't know him, so he didn't like him.

"Give me a good cigar," called Hopkins happily.

Mr. Freshmayer wasn't happy, but he brought him a cigar.

Hopkins lit it and began to smoke. Then he looked for some money, but he didn't have any.

"I don't have any money now, my friend," said Hopkins. "I'll pay you later." He started to leave the store.

Freshmayer was happy when he heard this. "I was right!" he thought. "I don't know this man, and now he doesn't want to pay me!"

He didn't say a word. He ran after Hopkins and kicked him hard. Hopkins didn't like this, so he hit him in the eye. His cigar was in his mouth. They moved out into the street and fought. People stopped and watched.

Of course, a policeman came. Hopkins was a nice, quiet person. He liked to stay at home in the evening and read. He didn't like to fight, but now he was angry.

They fought in front of a food store. Hopkins hit the policeman hard, and the policeman fell into some boxes of fruit and vegetables. He broke a big box of eggs. Then Hopkins hit Freshmayer again hard. "Next time," Freshmayer thought, "the customer can pay me later!"

Hopkins quickly ran away down the street. The policeman and Freshmayer ran behind him. There was egg on the policeman's coat.

Then Hopkins saw a long, fast red car in the street. The driver called to him, "Jump in!" Hopkins ran to the car and jumped in. The inside of the car was red too. It flew away down the street as quickly as a bird. The driver wore a dark blue jacket. He drove quickly and he didn't say a word.

"Thank you, my friend," said Hopkins. "Did you see the two men behind me? They almost caught me."

The driver didn't answer. Hopkins sat quietly and smoked his cigar. Ten minutes later, the car arrived in front of a large brown house. The driver got out.

"Come quickly," he said. "Miss Long will talk to you. She wants help. I'd like to help her, but she never asks me. No, I'm only a driver."

The driver took Hopkins into the house and then into a small room. A beautiful young woman stood up when they came in. Her face was unhappy and her eyes were angry.

"Miss Long," said the driver, "I went to Mr. Long's house. He wasn't there, so I came back. On the way, I saw this man. He was in a big fight, with ten, or twenty, or thirty men! They were policemen! He hit one, or three, or eight policemen! Mr. Long wasn't home, so I brought this man. He can help you!"

"Thank you, Armand," said the young woman. "You can go." She turned to Hopkins.

"I sent my driver to my brother's house because I want help. There's a man in this house. He's very unkind to me. When I talk to my aunt about this, she laughs at me. Armand says that you're strong. There aren't very many kind, strong men here in the City. Will you help me?"

John Hopkins put down his cigar. He looked at the beautiful young woman, and he fell in love for the first time.

He didn't forget the apartment, or the old dog, or his wife. This was different. This wonderful person wanted his help, and he couldn't say no.

"Show me the man!" he said. "I don't usually fight, but I'm enjoying it tonight!"

The young woman showed him a door. "He's in there," she said. "Are you afraid?"

"Me?" said John Hopkins. "Give me a flower from your hair." She gave him a red, red flower. He put it inside his coat, next to his heart.

He opened the door and walked into a room full of books. A young man sat in an armchair with a book in his hand.

He looked at the beautiful young woman, and he fell in love for the first time.

"Do you like to study?" Hopkins asked loudly. "Come here, and I'll give you a lesson! Then you won't be unkind to people!"

The young man was surprised. He stood up and quickly caught John Hopkins's arms. He took him to the front door of the house.

"Be careful, Ralph!" cried the young woman. "Don't hurt him! He's very kind! He only wanted to help me!"

The young man carefully pushed John Hopkins outside the door and then closed it.

"Bess," he said quietly. "You read too many stories. How did that man get in here?"

"Armand brought him," she answered. "I think you're very unkind! You don't want to buy me that nice big dog! I sent Armand for my brother. I was very angry with you."

The young man took her arm. "Listen, Bess," he said. "Think about it. That dog's very dangerous. He has very big teeth, and he likes to hurt people. Of course I don't want to buy him for you. All right? Now, let's tell your aunt that we're friends again."

Arm in arm, they moved away.

John Hopkins walked to his apartment. The neighbor's five-year-old daughter sat outside. Hopkins gave her a nice red flower and walked upstairs.

Mrs. Hopkins looked at him, but she wasn't interested. "Did you get your cigar?" she asked.

"Yes, I did," he answered. "And I went for a little trip around town. It's a nice night."

He sat down with a smile in the big armchair, and took out his cigar. He lit it again, and looked at the picture on the wall.

"Do you remember?" he said to his wife. "I started to tell you about Mr. Whipple's new coat. It's light gray, and it looks really nice."

"I started to tell you about Mr. Whipple's new coat."

Luck

Mark Twain

I first saw the famous man in London. There was a big dinner for him. Hundreds of people came and listened to him. I won't say his name. You will understand this when I tell you the story. I'll call him General Arthur Scoresby.

I first heard his name when he was an officer in the Crimean War. After that war he was famous and I heard his name thousands of times.

And there he was. The great man was really there. I was very interested in him, so I watched him carefully. I looked at his face again and again. It was quiet and strong. It was a good face, and I liked it.

All eyes were on him; they loved him. He wasn't the same as other famous people. He didn't look around the room. He didn't smile at the other people. He sat there quietly, and I liked him for that.

I knew the man next to me at the dinner. He taught in an army college when he was younger. He watched me with a strange light in his eyes when I looked at the General. He laughed and spoke quietly to me. "He's the most stupid man in the world!" he said.

I was very surprised. But I thought, "My friend's a good man, and he's intelligent. He understands other people very well. So he's right and we're all wrong. General Scoresby really isn't a great man." But how did my friend know that? Why didn't everybody know?

Two or three days later, I saw my friend again. This is his story.

I first saw the famous man in London.

"I first met young Scoresby in Woolwich. I was a teacher in an army college and he was in my class. The other students were smart. They answered my questions quickly and intelligently. But Scoresby didn't know anything. He always gave stupid answers to my questions. He was always wrong.

"I felt sad about this. He was a good boy, and everybody liked him. 'He'll do very badly in his tests,' I thought. 'I'll help him. But it won't change anything. He won't do very well, so he'll have to leave the college.'

"Every year, they ask the same questions in the test. We talked about those questions, and I told him the answers. Then I asked him the questions and he answered them. We studied the same questions again and again. He repeated the answers.

"And what happened? He did very well! Everybody was very happy. 'Good work!' they said to Scoresby. Other students knew more, but they did badly. It was an accident. This doesn't happen very often. He knew every question in the test. It was very good luck.

"The second test was more difficult. 'Do you understand this work?' I asked him. He didn't understand anything! 'I don't want him to feel stupid, so I'll help him again,' I thought. 'It's not important. The test will be too hard for him. This time he'll have to leave the college.'

"We did the same as before. We studied the same questions again and again, and he repeated the answers. He took the test. And what happened? His test was the best in the class! The other students knew more than Scoresby, so why was he the best? I don't know. I only helped him because I wanted to be kind. That was a big mistake.

"I thought about it day and night. I didn't sleep for a week. 'Oh, no!' I thought. 'Everybody thinks that he's wonderful. Now he'll get an important job! But he's too stupid! He won't do the job right! Everything will go wrong! What can I do? Why did I help him?' I felt very bad.

"Then the Crimean War started. 'This is bad luck!' I thought. 'Why did the war start now? Why not after Scoresby's dead? He'll make a lot of mistakes in a war.'

"I waited for something bad to happen, and it happened. They told me about it at the college. 'Scoresby's an officer now!' they said.

"'Oh, no!' I thought. 'Not Scoresby! He's the wrong man for the job. An officer has to be intelligent. Scoresby doesn't know anything! And he's too young! It's too dangerous! Everything will go wrong!' My hair almost turned white when I thought about it.

"Remember that it was my problem. But now it was also my country's problem. I had to do something, so I went away to war with Scoresby.

"And what happened there? He did the wrong thing every time, but the other officers didn't know that. When he made a mistake, they said, 'That was a good idea! That was very intelligent!' I didn't say anything.

"He got more and more famous. I was very angry. There was nothing inside his head! I knew that, but the other men didn't. I was also afraid. 'Now they'll give him a more important job!' I thought. 'Now he'll make bigger mistakes!'

"And I was right. Many other officers died in the war, so Scoresby climbed higher in the army. I was more and more afraid. 'How high will he go?' I thought. 'It'll be very bad when he falls. And I know that he'll fall!' Then he made his biggest mistake.

"Our men fought well that day, but it looked bad. 'We're losing!' I thought. 'We can't make any mistakes or we'll die!'

"An officer shouted. 'Scoresby! Take your men back there, to the right!'"

"An officer shouted. 'Scoresby! Take your men back there, to the right!'

"But Scoresby shouted to his men, 'Follow me! Into the woods!'

"I was very surprised. I thought, 'What's he doing? Where's he going? There's nobody there!'

"But we all ran into the woods behind Scoresby. And was there anybody there? Only the Russian army! All of them! And what happened? Did they kill us all? No. And why not? I'll tell you.

"The Russians thought, 'Oh, no, the English army know that we're here!' So they ran away, and we followed them. We won!

"The most important general in the English army was there, and he saw everything. He was very surprised and happy, and he went to see Scoresby. He spoke to him in front of everybody. And he gave him a medal!

"What was Scoresby's mistake that time? They wanted him to go back and turn right. But he went into the woods and turned left. *We* know that right is different from left. Scoresby didn't know that. It was only a small mistake.

"After that mistake, he was very famous. Everybody said, 'Isn't he wonderful? Isn't he intelligent? Isn't he a great man?' Again, I didn't say anything. What could I say?

"He's good, and he's kind. And he's the most stupid man in the world. But only three people know that. He knows. You know. And I know. But I know another thing. He also has the best luck in the world! When he makes a mistake, he gets another medal. He has hundreds of medals!

"So what does that mean? In this world, a man doesn't have to be intelligent. Luck is more important.

"And that's Scoresby's story. He's the most stupid man in the world, but he was born with luck!"

The Tell-Tale Heart

Edgar Allan Poe

Yes, I was often very afraid. I often feel the same way now. I jump at every little sound. But don't say that I'm crazy. When I was sick, my ears were very good. I heard everything very well. I heard the good things and the bad things. So how am I crazy? Look at me! Listen! I'll tell you the story nicely. I'm not a crazy person.

The idea came into my head and then it stayed there. Why? I don't know. It was with me day and night. I wasn't angry. I loved the old man. He never did anything wrong. He never said anything bad. I didn't want his money.

Was it his eye? Yes, it was! It was the same as a bird's eye. The inside of the eye was light blue. The outside was as white as milk. When it looked at me, I felt cold. What could I do? Slowly, I knew. I had to kill the old man. I wanted the eye to go away.

Listen to me! You think I'm crazy. Crazy people don't know anything. But you don't know *me*. You didn't see *me*. I planned everything. Nobody saw anything.

I was very kind to the old man before I killed him. And every night at around midnight, I waited at his door. I closed my lantern so it was dark. No light shone out from it. Then I opened the door quietly, and put the lantern in through the door. Then I put my head in. Isn't that funny? I was very smart. I wasn't crazy!

I moved very, very slowly. I didn't want to wake up the old man. After an hour, my head was inside the door. Is a crazy person as smart as that?

When my head was inside the door, I saw him in his bed. Then I opened the lantern very, very carefully. I didn't make any noise. A thin line of light came out and fell onto the bird's eye.

I did this for seven long nights. I did it every night, an hour before midnight. The eye was never open, so I didn't do the job. I didn't hate the old man. I hated his ugly bird's eye.

Every morning, I went into his room when the sun came up. I said, "Good morning! How are you? Did you sleep well?" I watched him every night, but he didn't know that. He wasn't very intelligent.

On the eighth night, I was very careful. I opened the door very slowly. My hand moved as slowly as the minute hand of a watch. I was happy. I was strong and he was weak. I wanted to laugh. I was in the old man's room, and he didn't know anything! He had no idea! Only I knew. I laughed at the idea. Maybe he heard me, because he moved suddenly in the bed. Did I stop? What do you think? No, I didn't.

His room was as black as night. No light came in through the windows. He couldn't see the door and I knew that. I pushed it slowly, slowly. Then I started to open the lantern, but the lantern door made a little noise. The old man sat up suddenly. "Who's there?" he cried.

I didn't move, and I said nothing. For one long hour I didn't move and he didn't move. I stood and listened. He sat up in his bed and listened. Night after night I listened, and now he listened too.

He made a noise. I knew that noise. He was afraid and I knew it. He wasn't hurt or sad. He was afraid for his life. It came from inside him when he heard me.

I knew this sound very well. There were many nights when I felt afraid. It always happened around midnight. Sometimes I too made this sound.

Yes, I knew it well. He felt afraid, and I was sad about that. At the same time, I laughed at him. He woke up when he heard the first noise. I knew that. Now he was more afraid.

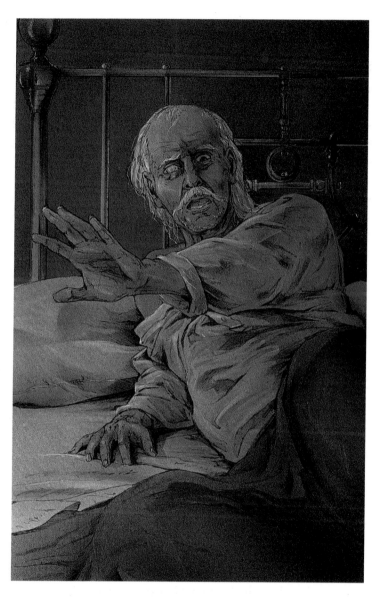

The old man sat up suddenly. "Who's there?" he cried.

He asked questions inside his head. "What was that? What made that noise?" Then he answered his questions. "It's the wind. It's a little animal. It's nothing."

He wanted to think that. He didn't want to feel afraid, but it was too late. Something was in his room, and it was very near him. He couldn't see it or hear it. He felt it when my head came into the dark room.

I waited for a long time. Then slowly, very slowly, I began to open the lantern again. A little light shone out weakly, and it fell onto the ugly blue and white bird's eye. The eye was wide, wide open! I looked at it, and I felt angry. I hated it! I felt cold all over my body. I couldn't see the old man's face or his body. How did I do it? I don't know. I shone the light only on his eye.

Some people hear and see very well. You think they're crazy. We talked about that. But you're wrong. They aren't crazy. I told you that too. I could hear very well, but I wasn't crazy.

A quick, quiet sound came to my ears. It wasn't as loud as a watch, but it was the same sound. It was the old man's heart. When I heard the sound, I got angrier. When I felt angry, I didn't feel afraid.

I didn't move, and I didn't move the lantern. I shone the light on the eye. The sound of the heart got louder. It got quicker and louder every minute. "He's really afraid now," I thought.

I'm often afraid. I told you that. I was there in that dark, old house. It was late at night, and it was very quiet. Then I heard this strange sound. It was the old man's heart! I was very afraid. I didn't move. Then the sound got louder. "Oh, no!" I thought. "The neighbors will hear it!" The old man had to die.

I shouted loudly and opened the lantern. Then I jumped into the room. The old man gave a scream—only one scream. I quickly pulled him onto the floor, and then I pulled the heavy bed over him. I smiled happily. "That's one half of the job," I thought.

But the heart didn't stop. I could hear it. I didn't feel afraid because the neighbors couldn't hear it through the wall. Then it stopped. The old man was dead. I pulled the bed off him, and I looked at his dead body. Yes, he was dead. I put my hand on his heart and left it there. There was nothing. He was dead. I wasn't afraid of his eye now.

Do you really think I'm crazy? Listen to me, and you won't think that. I had to do something with the body. I had to be very careful.

I didn't have a lot of time before the morning, so I worked quickly, but quietly. First, I cut up the body. I cut off the head, the arms, and the legs. Then I pulled up the floor. I put everything into the place under the floor, then I carefully put the floor back. It looked the same as before. Nobody's eyes could see anything different. And *his* eye couldn't see anything now.

Everything was clean. I was very careful, so I didn't have to wash anything. I was too smart. I want to laugh when I think about it.

I finished my work at four o'clock. It was as dark as midnight. Then I heard somebody at the door to the street. I went down and opened it with a smile. I wasn't afraid of anything.

Three policemen stood outside. I invited them into the house. They were there because a neighbor heard a scream in the night. Something was wrong, so he told the police. Now they wanted to look inside the house.

I smiled again. What was I afraid of? Nothing. I told my story. "I screamed in my sleep. I often do that. I'm the only person in

Three policemen stood outside.

the house. The old man is away in the country." I took the policemen through the house. "Please look *here*, and *here*," I said. "Please look *well*."

After some time, I took them to *his* room, and I showed them his money. It was all there. I really wasn't afraid. I brought some chairs into the room. "Please sit down," I said. I sat down happily, with my chair over the old man's body.

The policemen were happy too. They had the answer to their question. I wasn't afraid, so everything looked all right. We sat and talked about many things.

But then I started to feel weak. I felt the color leave my face. My head hurt, and there was a noise in my ears. The police stayed and talked. I spoke loudly, but the noise in my ears didn't stop. After some time, I knew. It wasn't inside my ears.

Now there was no color in my face. I spoke quickly, and loudly again. The noise was very loud too. What could I do? It was a quick, quiet sound. *It made the same sound as a watch, but quieter.*

The policemen couldn't hear it. I spoke fast and loudly again. The noise got louder. I stood up and talked again. What did I talk about? I don't know. I had to say something because of the noise. It was very loud.

Why didn't the policemen go? I walked up and down heavily. My feet made a lot of noise on the floor. I spoke angrily, but the noise was always there.

The men watched me. I didn't want to look afraid. I talked loudly and angrily. I used bad language, and I shouted crazily. I moved my chair across the floor. It made a loud noise, but the other noise was louder. It got louder and louder and *louder!*

The men smiled and talked in a friendly way. Didn't they hear it? Yes, of course they heard it! They *knew!* They laughed at me because I was afraid. I thought that then, and I think it now.

"Pull up the floor! Look here!"

I couldn't wait! I had to stop their smiles! They weren't friendly smiles. I didn't want them to laugh at me. I had to tell them or die! The noise got louder, louder, *louder!*

"Stop it!" I shouted. "Don't smile at me! I know that you know. I did it! Pull up the floor! Look here! Listen! It's the sound of his ugly old heart!"

ACTIVITIES

A White Heron

Before you read

1 Find these words in your dictionary. They are all in the story. Make sentences with the words.
   a *heron   nest   branch*
   b *cow   whistle*
   c *surprised   heart*

After you read

2 Answer these questions.
   a Who does Sylvia meet in the woods? Why is he there?
   b Why does Sylvia climb the big tree?
   c Her grandmother and the young man ask her a question when she comes home. What is it? Why doesn't she answer?
   d Why does Sylvia feel sad at the end of the story?

3 Work with another student. Have this conversation.
   Student A: You are the grandmother. You want Sylvia to answer the young man's question.
   Student B: You are Sylvia. You don't want to tell them the answer.

4 Does Sylvia do the right thing? What do you think?

The Story of an Hour and **The Complete Life of John Hopkins**

Before you read

5 How can a person's life change in an hour? Think of some ways.
6 Read these sentences. What do the words in *italics* mean? Look in your dictionary.
   a He bought a *cigar* and smoked it on the way home.
   b Is this the *complete* story or only half of it?
   c She was very *poor*, but then she married a rich man.
   d I *screamed* when I saw his *body* on the ground.
   e We lost two sons in the *war*.

7 Answer these questions about *The Story of an Hour*.

  a What does Josephine tell her sister?

  b Why does Mrs. Mallard want to have a long life?

  c How did she feel the day before? Why?

  d What happens to Mrs. Mallard at the end of the story? Why?

8 Are these sentences about John Hopkins right or wrong? Change the wrong sentences.

  a Hopkins lives in a big city.

  b He is a poor man.

  c He pays for a cigar.

  d A policeman hits him.

  e He helps a beautiful young woman.

  f He fights with a young man.

  g He is unhappy when he goes back home.

9 Which of the two stories is more interesting, do you think?

Luck and The Tell-Tale Heart

Before you read

10 Find these words in your dictionary:

  army   general   lantern   luck   medal   officer   tell-tale

  a Which words are about war?

  b Which is a word for a light?

  c What do you think these two stories are about?

After you read

11 Tell the story of Scoresby's first medal in *Luck*. Number the sentences.

  a An English general gives Scoresby a medal.

  b They find the Russian army.

  c He takes his men into the woods and turns left.

  d An officer tells Scoresby, "Take your men back there, to the right."

  e The Russian army runs away.

  f Scoresby says to his men, "Follow me!"

12 Finish these sentences. Tell the story of *The Tell-Tale Heart*.

    a The writer visits the old man's room at night because ...

    b He closes the lantern so ...

    c He puts the lantern into the old man's room before ...

    d The old man can't see him but ...

    e He pulls the old man onto the floor and ...

    f He puts the old man's body under the floor after ...

    g He talks loudly when he ...

    h He has to tell the police because ...

13 Discuss these questions: Who is telling the story of *The Tell-Tale Heart*? Who is he talking to? Where is he?

Writing

14 You are the young man in *A White Heron*. Write a letter to your family. What happened at Mrs. Tilley's house? Tell them.

15 You are John Hopkins. Write about the day in the story. How do you feel at the end of the day?

16 Write about General Scoresby's life. Where did he study? Was he a good student? What did he do later?

17 You are a policeman in *The Tell-Tale Heart*. You went to the old man's house that night. What happened then and later?

Answers for the Activities in this book are published in our free resource packs for teachers, the Penguin Readers Factsheets, or available on a separate sheet. Please write to your local Pearson Education office or to: Marketing Department, Penguin Longman Publishing, 5 Bentinck Street, London W1M 5RN.